fund-raising event.

"*Dave Swarbrick and his Fairport buddy Dave Pegg have recruited former group member Simon Nicol for a special charity gig at Prescott Manor Farm, Cropredy, near Banbury*", said the first paragraph of the short item in the music press.

Also on the bill were:

Bob Davenport: source of Hexhamshire Lass and one of Britain's most revered traditional singers. According to some accounts he was considered as Sandy's replacement in 1970.

John Golding: singer/songwriter, most recent album '*Photographs*'.

Cats Cradle: local band. The event started at 6.00pm, "'til late", with tickets available from 3 Vicarage Gardens; they cost £1.

The event is significant, not just because it could be considered the first Cropredy Festival (which is really stretching the point a little), but also because it brought Simon back into the fold. But this small event unwittingly

s
s
w
C
n

———— ❖ ————

❝ *We've never set ourselves apart from the punters, never ignored what the fans say. When we walk around the field at Cropredy, we see so many people we recognise. Those you don't know by name, you know by sight. And it's great to see them bringing their friends and families too* ❞ **Simon Nicol**

———— ❖ ————

Over the years that initial 750 has grown to over 20,000, drawn not just from the *local* community but from the vast *Fairport* community, all around the whole world.

This booklet is a souvenir and celebration of the world's finest village fête.

My FIRST EXPERIENCE of Cropredy, and of Fairport, came about by accident. In 1977 (I was 17) a friend of mine and his girlfriend had been bought tickets in advance. As my friend couldn't go, his girlfriend, I'll call her H, asked if I'd like to go with her. Four of us travelled to Cropredy, me, H, her brother driving and his mate.

The arena appeared to be a large lawn to the rear of someone's large house. I can't remember any of the acts that were on during the day nor the exact whereabouts of this large lawn! - but I do remember there was trouble with the power as a call was put out from the stage for anyone who might know anything about diesel-powered generators. Someone sat on a hay bale near me swayed to his feet, slurred "I'll have a look", and was taken through a hole in the hedge, stage right! A few moments later power was restored and the unlikely hero returned to much applause.

Sometime in the afternoon I noticed a small figure in a large hairy jacket moving through the crowd smiling and greeting people. I asked H who it was and she told me it was Dave Swarbrick.

Before Fairport came on I thought I'd relieve myself of some of the ale I'd been drinking throughout the day. At the back of the lawn/arena was a handful of toilet cubicles and,

behind these, a stream. As the toilets were all occupied, it had to be the stream, and I remember standing on the bank looking up- and down-stream and laughing out loud. There were scores of us, like an army of anglers, all stood there with our tackle in our hands!

Fairport were terrific, the high point for me being the incredible 'Bonny Bunch of Roses' and I was converted on the spot. (Although the real high point came on the journey home when, in the back of the car while her brother drove, H and myself got very friendly - but that's another story!)

After my first Cropredy I vowed to return, and return I did - 23 years later, in August 2000 with my partner, my brother and his wife. And we have made another vow: To continue returning, every year, for as long as Fairport do. **GrogZep**

1978

MY FIRST CROPREDY was in 1978 with the show in the garden of Prescott Manor. Earlier that day there was a village fete where, if memory serves, Ralph McTell tried to win a goldfish. Many less people in those days – about 500 at the gig – and guests included Earl Okin, Ian Campbell Folk Group, then Ralph McTell, and Trevor Lucas with Fairport. I recall a fight breaking out right in front when Fairport were playing and Dave Swarbrick stopping the music to tell them to pack it in. "It's not a bloody Rolling Stones concert." **Graham Warren**

THESE DAYS I can point the car south and I think it knows how to find Cropredy. Back in 1978, I spent days planning a route to this strange little dot on the map I had never heard off. There had been tales of the previous two years' village fetes: a friend of mine had gone along just because she was in the area. This year I was determined to make a special effort. I had expected something like the festivals of the early seventies.

Instead I found a welcoming English village, its streets lined with stalls in a way which positively resisted any automotive influx. I found a place to park and went for a wander, eventually finding someone who knew where "the pop group" would be playing. The concert took place on a stage for which the word makeshift would be a euphemism and was a real old meets new. The Ian Campbell Group of which both Peggy and Swarb had been members were on fine form: Fairport themselves aided and abetted by Ralph McTell and Trevor Lucas. Wish I'd kept a note of what they played. I remember Polly On The Shore, White Dress and Rosie... and Trev remarking that the gig had the poshest backstage area he'd ever seen. **Joel Evans**

1979

'MY FIRST CROPREDY?? - that would have to be 1979. Can't remember much about it, must have be the beer. My mate Mike drove me down (or maybe it was Sam, 22 years is a long time) - and we parked and wandered through a field of tents, to another field full of long-haired freaky people, short-haired folky people, and all shades between.

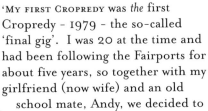

The band jetted (!) in from Knebworth and were away. I seem to remember Swarb was on great form, but my abiding memory is of the compère announcing the second encore with "this is the first time they've played this one for years, and you know that they won't follow it with another" - then the band launched into an emotional Meet On The Ledge, and the audience sang out with tears in their eyes.

After all, this was their farewell concert, this was the last song they were ever going to sing. Ever.

Or so we thought at the time!'

Bob Brock

'MY FIRST CROPREDY was *the* first Cropredy - 1979 - the so-called 'final gig'. I was 20 at the time and had been following the Fairports for about five years, so together with my girlfriend (now wife) and an old school mate, Andy, we decided to make the journey to Cropredy to pay our respects at the passing of a great band. In those days we were poor students, so this meant a number of train connections starting from Croydon. I remember the journey well - Andy's father had worked for the railways so he had cashed-in one of his 'free ticket' allowances and received in the post a return ticket from Croydon to Cropredy. This rather amused the conductor on the train from Oxford who told us that 'there's not been a station at Cropredy for forty years'.

So we left the train at Banbury and caught a taxi. When we told the driver where we wanted to go and why he immediately got onto 'base' and warned them to 'get a few more cabs down to the station pronto, as there appeared to be a bit of a do on at Cropredy'. - and 22 years later we're still rolling up, but these days in a people carrier full of camping gear and children - and Andy's still waiting for the train service to include an extra stop at Cropredy that weekend.'

Doug Stammers

THE Fairport Convention NEWS
FINAL EDITION

GROUP DISBANDS
✳SENSATION✳

FAREWELL CONCERT IN
CROPREDY

SATURDAY 4TH AUGUST 1979 4.00 P.M

READ THE FULL EXCLUSIVE

**EARL OKIN
STEVE ASHLEY
CHRIS LESLIE
PLUS MANY
SUPPORT
BANDS**

**FAREWELL
FAREWELL**
THE COMMEMORATIVE ALBUM
FROM FAIRPORT CONVENTION
£4.00
FROM, WOODWORM RECORDS
CHAPEL ROW, CROPREDY
NR. BANBURY, OXON

REFRESHMENTS, LICENSED BAR. CAR PARKING AVAILABLE 30p PLUS MANY STALLS.

ADMISSION BY PROGRAMME ONLY. PRICE £2.50 (£3.00 ON THE DAY). APPLY WITH REMITTANCE &
LARGE S.A.E. TO J. HEAVERMAN, VICARAGE GARDENS, CROPREDY, NR BANBURY, OXON.

1980

NOT MY FIRST CATERING-CROPREDY...
I'd been interested in the band since
the late 60s thanks to friends like
Bern from Sydney, John Penhallow,
Kingsley Abbott and the Sydney
Friends of Fairport. (I paid a huge
amount of money (in those days) to
attend Emmanuel College May Ball
when they played in June 1973).
I started my catering work in 1980
and wrote to Chris Pegg to ask if I
might be involved in the "first
annual reunion" on August 30th
that year. She wrote back and, in the
nicest possible way, doubted that
there would be sufficient demand for
vegetarian food. I attended anyway.

It was a spectacular evening in
every way, but the queues at the food
vendors suggested that Chris may
just have been wrong. She agreed
and said I would be in next year, the
start of a long association with the
festival, the band, Cropredy and
everything else that flows from the
most exciting weekend of each year. I
still have the Melody Maker report by
Colin Irwin in which he quotes Dave
Pegg "I think we might do it again
next year. Everybody had a good
time... We all enjoyed playing –
there's a lot of electricity and
spontaneity when you haven't played
together for a year. Nobody really
knew what was going to happen and
that's always half the fun" **Leon**

MY WIFE FRANCES AND I were at the
first Cropredy reunion on 30th
August 1980. These notes are from
the diary I wrote that day:
"A pleasant drive up to Cropredy,

and we managed to
set up the tents before
it began to rain. Only
trouble was that we
hadn't enough tents for
Wendy to have one to
herself: though sensitive
about this, she eventually
arranged to share Ian's!
Excellent concert! Really moving to
see RT with them after so many
years. It finished with the band,
Mattacks, the Thompsons and
McTell, singing all sorts of songs
together. Wonderful, and I had my
first puff of a joint!" **Steve Royston**

WITH MY USUAL impeccable sense of
timing, my interest in Fairport
began on the day they broke up. I
was only 13 years old but already a
confirmed fan of Jethro Tull. One
hot August day Radio 1 interviewed
Dave Pegg about the group's
imminent demise and he revealed
that he was about to join Ian
Anderson and chums. A few weeks
later I invested in *Farewell Farewell*, *Liege
& Lief*, *Bonny Bunch* etc. As the months
went by my fascination for the group
grew and along with it my sadness
that I had missed them 'live'.
Imagine, then, my absolute delight
when word filtered through that they
were going to reform for a one-off
bash at Cropredy. 21 years later I
can't remember an awful lot about
that day other than the changeable
weather, Richard & Linda
Thompson and the euphoria that
greeted the band's arrival on stage.
Carey Hancock

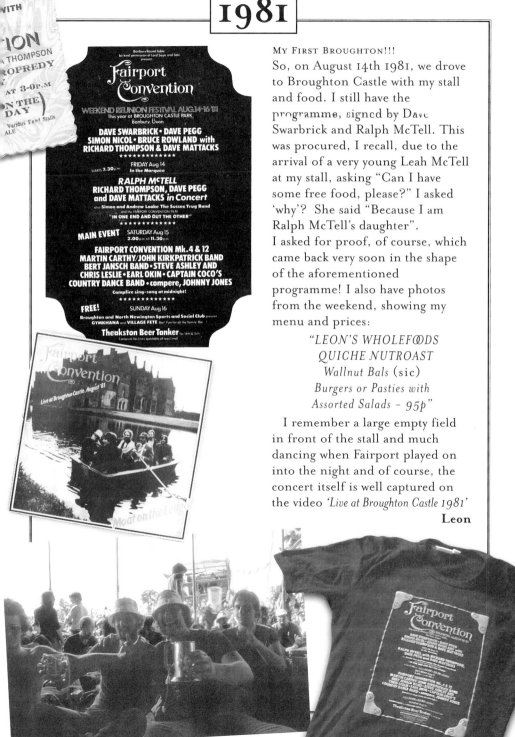

My First Broughton!!!

So, on August 14th 1981, we drove to Broughton Castle with my stall and food. I still have the programme, signed by Dave Swarbrick and Ralph McTell. This was procured, I recall, due to the arrival of a very young Leah McTell at my stall, asking "Can I have some free food, please?" I asked 'why'? She said "Because I am Ralph McTell's daughter".

I asked for proof, of course, which came back very soon in the shape of the aforementioned programme! I also have photos from the weekend, showing my menu and prices:

> *"LEON'S WHOLEFOODS*
> *QUICHE NUTROAST*
> *Wallnut Bals (sic)*
> *Burgers or Pasties with*
> *Assorted Salads - 95p"*

I remember a large empty field in front of the stall and much dancing when Fairport played on into the night and of course, the concert itself is well captured on the video *'Live at Broughton Castle 1981'*

Leon

1982

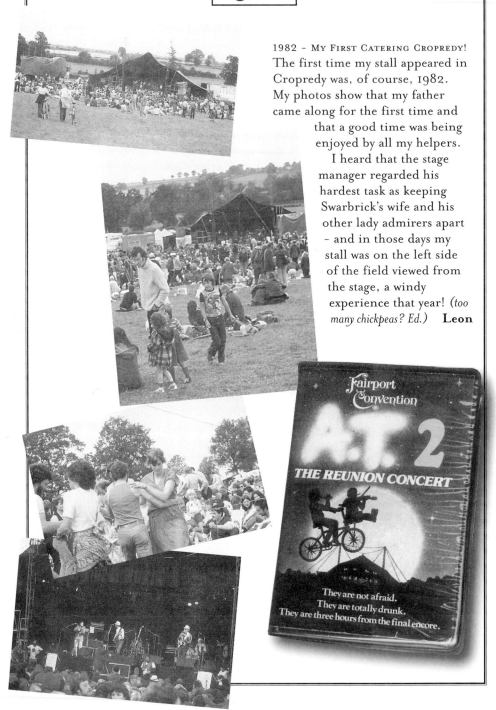

1982 – MY FIRST CATERING CROPREDY! The first time my stall appeared in Cropredy was, of course, 1982. My photos show that my father came along for the first time and that a good time was being enjoyed by all my helpers.

I heard that the stage manager regarded his hardest task as keeping Swarbrick's wife and his other lady admirers apart – and in those days my stall was on the left side of the field viewed from the stage, a windy experience that year! *(too many chickpeas? Ed.)* **Leon**

·A WEEKEND IN THE COUNTRY·

Fairport Convention '82

Third Annual Reunion, Cropredy, 13/14 August 1982

SOUVENIR PROGRAMME

ENTER OUR COMPETITION AND WIN A BARREL OF **THEAKSTON'S BITTER!** SEE INSIDE FOR DETAILS

1983

THIS FIRST TIME that I went to Cropredy was special in many ways. In those days, Fairport only played together once a year, at the Festival – the anticipation was an exciting and wonderful feeling to experience. The weather was just perfect that year, and though attendance in those days was probably one-third of what it is today, everyone there truly loved this band, and it felt like a big gathering of friends.

Special guests that year included Ashley Hutchings, Richard Thompson, and Bruce Rowland: Cathy Le Surf sang the Sandy Denny songs, and Dave Swarbrick was in great form – and even though I've since been to eight other Cropredys, that first one was unforgettable.
Kenneth Wexler
Brooklyn, NY

AS I WRITE these recollections, I am listening to the CD of *"The Boot"*. I don't need to think back to what Fairport did or what they sounded like. Here it all is. As I recall, this was before the idea of wheeling on surprise guests really caught on and the programme clearly advised us to expect Ashley and Cathy LeSurf , RT and the twin drumming talents of Mattacks and Rowland.

The weather stayed fine. The crowd was the friendliest I had been part of. The music was superb. I remember being delighted to hear two songs from *"Rock On"* by The Bunch. An eccentric pleasure, perhaps but it's one of my favourite albums. Then there were all those songs from *"Liege and Lief"*. How could we have had any doubt that Fairport will survive? And aren't we glad they did! **C. Peter Knight** (no relation)

A WEEKEND IN THE COUNTRY

(Being the Fourth Annual Reunion of the Much Renowned

Fairport Convention

FEATURING

MR. DAVID SWARBRICK, MR. DAVID PEGG, MR. SIMON NICOL, MR. RICHARD THOMPSON, MR. DAVID MATTACKS, MR. BRUCE ROWLAND, MR. ASHLEY HUTCHINGS, MS. CATHY LESURF

ON

FRIDAY & SATURDAY, 12/13 AUGUST 1983

AT

HOME FARM, CROPREDY, NR BANBURY, OXON.

FULL SUPPORTING CAST INCLUDES

THE *

RICHARD THOMPSON BIG BAND

VIN GARBUTT

THE

ALBION BAND

MAXI & MITCH

THE ARIZONA SMOKE REVIEW

JON BENNS*

(*denotes artists appearing on Friday)

BLOWZABELLA CARRIG EVESDROPPER* ECLIPSE & SURPRISE GUESTS!!

REAL MUSIC, REAL BEER & REAL FOOD, AT UNREAL PRICES

TICKETS

FROM WOODWORM RECORDS *OR*
P.O. BOX 37, BANBURY
OXFORDSHIRE
(Please send S.A.E.)

IN ADVANCE

FRIDAY NIGHT (7.30 - 11.00)	£4.50
SATURDAY (2.00 - 12.00)	£6.50
WEEKEND TICKET	£10.00

CAMPING & CAR PARKING

(1982 concert recorded live — now available on C90 cassette, £5.50 inc. P&P. Write to Woodworm Records)

1984

THE PROGRAMME SAID it was the fifth annual Cropredy, but it seemed to have been going on for much longer than that. I'd always been keen on folk festivals...but had always dismissed Fairport as a rock band. It was the line up that attracted me, not Fairport, I must admit. Bob Davenport, Ian Campbell. A second chance to see Whippersnapper. Battlefield Band, The Oysters, Pyewackett and Steeleye. I remember remarking that it was worth the ticket even with seeing Fairport. In fact I had planned to beat an early retreat and avoid the traffic.

I was there on my own but in the way of things I made friends over the weekend. They convinced me that I should stay and "see at least some of the set". It was the best advice I have ever had. I stayed to the end, became an immediate Fairport Con-vert and have been to every Cropredy since, with no thought of leaving early. So has my wife whom I met that weekend!   **Ian Peterson**

I MUST CONFESS to having stopped buying Fairport LPs in the mid seventies. However, I remember my eye being caught by a poster for the 1984 Cropredy. So many of the names seemed to hail from the sixties folk revival (my era!). The fact that Fairport were playing was almost an added bonus. When it came down to it, though, I recall the set was spell binding. There were Fairport classics, but these were interspersed with other hits - I particularly recall 'Day Trip To Bangor', a recent chart topper, and Richard Thompson doing 'Bright Lights Tonight'.

But most of all what sticks in my mind is being close to a crowd of young Fairport fans. Aside from the fact I was amazed that such beings existed, they provided me with the opportunity to display my superior knowledge ad identify the Campbells, Bob Davenport and others when they came on stage.

Steph Parsonage

THE FIFTH ANNUAL REUNION,

FRIDAY 10th & SATURDAY 11th AUGUST, 1984
AT CROPREDY Nr BANBURY, OXFORDSHIRE

Fairport Convention

Featuring Dave Swarbrick, Dave Pegg, Simon Nicol,
Richard Thompson, Dave Mattacks and Bruce Rowland.
With guests Cathy Lesurf, Wally Whyton,
Ian & Lorna Campbell and Bob Davenport. PLUS:

STEELEYE SPAN

ADRIAN LEGG
ALLAN TAYLOR
THE BATTLEFIELD BAND
GARSTERS DREAM BAND
HALLS OXFORD CONCERT BRASS
THE OYSTER BAND
PYEWACKETT
RAGGED HEROES
RICHARD DIGANCE
WHIPPERSNAPPER

GOOD FOOD, GOOD BEER, CAMPING, AMPLE CAR PARKING

TICKETS: *Before August 1st –* FRIDAY £5.00, SATURDAY £8.00, WEEKEND £11.00
After August 1st and on the day – FRIDAY £6.00, SATURDAY £9.00, WEEKEND £13.00
Available from: **WOODWORM RECORDS, P.O. BOX 37, BANBURY, OXON, OX15 4BH**

The only place to be on August 9 and 10, if you enjoy good beer and great music

CROPREDY

WADWORTH'S
great beers from the West Country

I DON'T REMEMBER MY FIRST VISIT to the Cropredy festival, since I was one year old at the time - but I've had the story relayed to me many a time. My parents were carrying me about for the entire weekend, and at some point they bumped into Simon Nicol at the bar; A conversation ensued, the result of which was the following dedication by Simon during Fairport's set that year:

"Here is a little dedication for somebody who's here this year and wasn't able to be here last year because they were busy being born at the time. So, for James Royston, if you're still out there - if your mummy and daddy will let you stay up this late on your first big outing - here is a number for you. It's actually a set of tunes about a subject which you're probably a bit of an expert on at the moment, being the average twelve month old child that you probably are. It's called Dirty Linen."

James Royston

MY FIRST CROPREDY was in 1985, although I'd been meaning to go since 1983. In those days the gig started at 6pm Friday: With no public transport from Banbury, it was five miles on 'shanks's pony'! Eighty-Five was a good Cropredy to attend, because Fairport played

Friday and Saturday, and DM and Richard turned up to recreate the Full House line-up. Their set included my favourite track, 'Sir B Mackenzie', and a classic 'Matty Groves'. Of the other acts, I remember being impressed by Neil Innes, and

shocked, stunned and totally amazed by surprise guest Billy Connolly, whose 'Two Little Boys In Blue' went down a storm with the two members of the Oxon Constabulary on duty.

In 1985, Cropredy was still a relatively small festival, so its friendliness wasn't really surprising. What is surprising is that it is still as friendly, in spite of how it's grown. It's certainly the only music festival I'd bother with, and I'm sure lots of others feel the same way. I attended my first Cropredy with my mate Phil, his mate John, and Phil's girlfriend's sister, Janice. If these words do make it into the 35th anniversary package, I'd like to dedicate them to Phil for creating the Fairport monster, or at least introducing me to it. **Steve Ducker**

LADIES AND GENTLEMEN

PRESENTING FOR YOUR DELECTATION AND DELIGHT

THE SIXTH ANNUAL REUNION OF

Fairport Convention

AT CROPREDY, Nr. BANBURY, OXFORDSHIRE

FRIDAY 9 AUGUST & SATURDAY 10 AUGUST

NINETEEN HUNDRED AND EIGHTY-FIVE

FEATURING FAIRPORT ON NO LESS THAN *BOTH NIGHTS!*

WITH A CAST INCLUDING

Mr. **David Swarbrick** . the Demon Fiddler
Messrs. **Simon Nicol** ⎫ Sundry
Richard Thompson ⎬ ..... Guitar
Jerry Donahue ⎭ Heroes
Mr. **Trevor Lucas** ... Antipodean Artistry

Mr. **David Pegg** .... the Cocktail Cowboy
Messrs. **David Mattacks** ⎱ .. those Paragons
Bruce Rowland ⎰ of the Paradiddle
Miss **Cathy Lesurf** ....
.... the Bangor Nightingale

ABLY SUPPORTED BY

THE BALHAM ALLIGATORS

THE HOME SERVICE

THE JOHN JAMES BAND

featuring Dick Heckstall-Smith

JON BENNS

MOSAIC

NEIL INNES*

NO RIGHT TURN*

ROBIN WILLIAMSON

WHIPPERSNAPPER

Please note ∗ *denotes Friday night appearance*

CAMPING

CAR PARKING

BAR , FOOD

MORRIS TEAMS

CHILDREN'S

ENTERTAINMENTS

ADVANCE TICKETS	FRIDAY £5.00 SATURDAY £9.00 WEEKEND £12.00	AFTER 1st AUGUST	FRIDAY £6.00 SATURDAY £10.00 WEEKEND £15.00

TICKETS FROM WOODWORM RECORDS, P.O. BOX 37, BANBURY, OXON, OX15 4BH

(PLEASE ENCLOSE STAMPED ADDRESSED ENVELOPE)

I WONDER HOW MANY other people still have their scanty panties? I have a dim recollection of being assured of their good value sometime during Saturday afternoon. One of our party — I forget who — disappeared for a pint and returned with a bagful. I guess the beer took effect, as it seemed a great idea at the time to wear them as hats during Fairport's set.

Yes - and we were the ones who thought it was funny to throw them at Robert Plant. Somehow a spare pair ended up in my rucksack, however, which took a little explaining to the wife when I arrived home on Sunday afternoon! **John The Gun**

AT CROPREDY · NR BANBURY · OXFORDSHIRE

– FRIDAY 8TH AUGUST · 7.00pm TILL 11.30pm –

THE RICHARD THOMPSON BAND

KIERAN HALPIN *with* **MARTIN ALLCOCK** *and* **MANUS LUNNY**
MIKE ELLIOTT

– SATURDAY 9TH AUGUST · 12.30pm TILL 11.30pm –

FAIRPORT CONVENTION

*with Simon Nicol, Dave Pegg, Dave Mattacks, Ric Sanders, Martin Allcock
plus Richard Thompson, Jerry Donahue, Ian Matthews and Cathy Lesurf*

BRASS MONKEY · DICK GAUGHAN · REDGUM *from Australia*
THE SUTHERLAND BROTHERS *with Mattacks, Pegg and Donahue*
THE ELECTRIC BLUEBIRDS · THE JON STRONG BAND · SURPRISE GUESTS!

MORRIS TEAMS · CHILDREN'S ENTERTAINMENT
REAL ALE AND THE BEST IN FESTIVAL FOOD · CAMPING · CRAFT STALLS

– SUNDAY 10TH AUGUST –

End-of-festival bash at Banbury Moat House Hotel with

FLACO JIMENEZ

(not included in festival ticket price – tickets available on site)

TICKETS

*Before July 25th – Weekend £13.00 · Friday £6.00 · Saturday £10.00
After July 25th – Weekend £16.00 · Friday £7.00 · Saturday £11.00
Children under 14 admitted FREE with accompanying adult*

FOR TICKETS AND INFORMATION, WRITE TO WOODWORM RECORDS
PO BOX 37 · BANBURY · OXFORDSHIRE OX15 4BH · ENGLAND

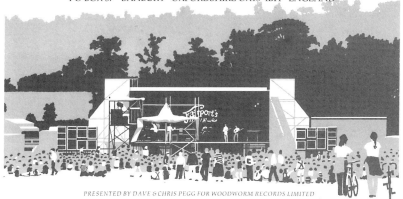

PRESENTED BY DAVE & CHRIS PEGG FOR WOODWORM RECORDS LIMITED

1987 WAS THE YEAR — one of the best ever for weather.

Outstanding memories (we've been every subsequent year — hope they're not muddled): pitching the tent on one of the crests of the medieval strip-farmed fields and spending the night constantly rolling downhill in one direction or the other; being allowed into the arena for the sound-check; hearing the sound of Simon's "Before Your time" (the "No Other" of the 1980s) being played between sets both days; the joy of finding good vegetarian and vegan food at Ricardo's and Leon's; John Martyn storming off stage and threatening to sort out the sound man; but what remains longest and strongest is the overall impression of a joyous assembly and the inspired performances that arise from the band as a consequence. Other than that, it's just a gig in a field.

Ian & Kim

MY FIRST CROPREDY WAS 1987 - I was completely entranced by the whole event! The great music, food, weather, but most of all the people and the atmosphere — all helped by the glorious weather. From that small seed has grown an annual pilgrimage. **Rod Hughes**

VENI, VIDI, IMBIBI

Fairport Convention

TWENTIETH ❧ ANNIVERSARY ❧ WEEKEND
❧ CROPREDY Nr. BANBURY OXFORDSHIRE ❧
FRIDAY 14 & SATURDAY 15 AUGUST 1987
* denotes artists appearing Friday night

IAN ANDERSON & MARTIN BARRE ❧
from Jethro Tull
MARTIN ALLCOCK ❧❧❧❧ THE STEVE
ASHLEY BAND ❧ CHICKEN SHACK ❧
JERRY DONAHUE ❧❧❧❧❧ GORDON
GILTRAP* ❧ LE RUE* ❧ CATHY LE SURF ❧
MARA ❧❧❧ JOHN MARTYN & DANNY
THOMPSON* ❧❧❧❧ DAVE MATTACKS ❧
RALPH McTELL ❧ MUZSIKÁS ❧ SIMON
NICOL ❧ DAVE PEGG ❧ RIC SANDERS ❧
DAVE SWARBRICK ❧❧ JUNE TABOR ❧
❧❧❧❧ RICHARD THOMPSON ❧❧❧❧
❧❧❧❧❧❧ WHIPPERSNAPPER ❧❧❧❧❧❧

The best in festival toilets, food and drink.
Elegantly sufficient camping and car parking.

TICKETS

Before 1st August: Weekend £14, Friday £6, Saturday £11.
After 1st August: Weekend £17, Friday £7, Saturday £12.
From Woodworm Records, PO Box 37, Banbury, Oxon OX15 4BH
Pay by Access, cheque or postal order. Please enclose SAE.

'THE ARISTOCRAT OF FESTIVALS'

PRESENTED BY DAVE & CHRIS PEGG FOR WOODWORM RECORDS LTD

My first Cropredy? Friends had been telling me to go for years. They played me the tapes, shown me the videos, made me read setlists, told me about guests. In 1988 I finally agreed. I was, I admit, lured by tales of Tull and Plant.

So this was not the best year to start. Expecting guest appearances from Rock Gods, all I got was an opera singer!

Mind you, it was an in-at-the-deep-end introduction to Fairport's music – and Richard Thompson's for that matter. The following year I was on the mailing list and I am proud to say I got my tickets before anyone else!

Brian Shackleton

Fairport Convention's 1988 Reunion

AT CROPREDY NR BANBURY OXON

Friday 12th August Saturday 13th August

FRIDAY 7.30p.m. - 11-30p.m.
COLLABORATION, MIKE SILVER AND THE RICHARD THOMPSON BAND.

SATURDAY 12.30p.m - 11.30p.m
THE KURSAAL FLYERS SALLY BARKER, FILARFOLKET, THE STEVE GIBBONS BAND, DIZ DIZLEY, THE DAN AR BRAS BAND FAIRPORT & GUESTS

TICKETS BEFORE 25TH JULY :- FRIDAY £8 SATURDAY £12 WEEKEND £17
AFTER 25TH JULY :- FRIDAY £9 SATURDAY £14 WEEKEND £20

REAL ALE, FOOD, CAMPING, MORRIS TEAMS, CHILDRENS ENTERTAINMENT. ACCOMPANIED CHILDREN UNDER 14 YEARS ADMITTED FREE

Commentary

Fairport Convention 1988

ANNUAL REUNION

SIMON NICOL
DAVE PEGG
DAVE MATTACKS
RIC SANDERS
MARTIN ALLCOCK
WITH GUESTS ▶
RICHARD THOMPSON
JERRY DONAHUE
SHEILA &
SHERYL PARKER
PLUS ▶
THE RICHARD
THOMPSON BAND*
DAN AR BRAS'
ELECTRIC BAND
MIKE SILVER*
THE STEVE
GIBBONS BAND
FILARFOLKET
THE KURSAAL FLYERS
COLLABORATION*
SALLY BARKER
DIZ DIZLEY

artists appearing Friday night

*Friday 12th August
7.30pm – 11.30pm*

*Saturday 13th August
1pm – 11.30pm*

*Home Farm, Cropredy
near Banbury, Oxfordshire*

*Tickets available
from Woodworm Records
PO Box 37, Banbury
Oxfordshire OX15 4BH*

*Before Monday 25th July:
Friday night – £8.00
Saturday – £12.00
Weekend – £17.00*

*After Monday 25th July:
Friday night – £9.00
Saturday – £14.00
Weekend – £20.00*

*Pay by Access, cheque or PO
Please enclose SAE.*

FREE camping and car park

*The best (as ever) in
festival toilets,
food and drink!*

Bar supplied by
WADWORTH'S

PRESENTED BY DAVE & CHRIS PEGG FOR WOODWORM RECORDS LTD

1989

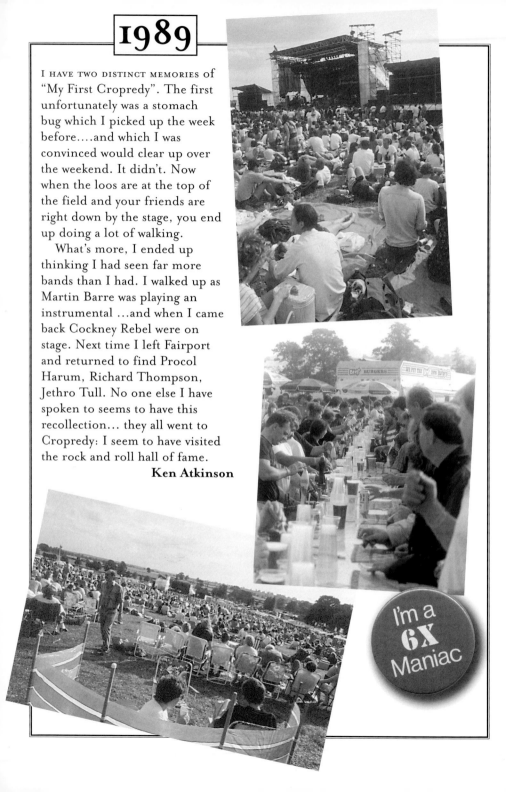

I HAVE TWO DISTINCT MEMORIES of "My First Cropredy". The first unfortunately was a stomach bug which I picked up the week before....and which I was convinced would clear up over the weekend. It didn't. Now when the loos are at the top of the field and your friends are right down by the stage, you end up doing a lot of walking.

What's more, I ended up thinking I had seen far more bands than I had. I walked up as Martin Barre was playing an instrumental ...and when I came back Cockney Rebel were on stage. Next time I left Fairport and returned to find Procol Harum, Richard Thompson, Jethro Tull. No one else I have spoken to seems to have this recollection... they all went to Cropredy: I seem to have visited the rock and roll hall of fame.

Ken Atkinson

I'm a
6X
Maniac

Fairport Convention

invite you to the

1989 CROPREDY FESTIVAL

FRIDAY 18 & SATURDAY 19 AUGUST

CROPREDY · NR BANBURY · OXFORDSHIRE

featuring

RICHARD THOMPSON
STEELEYE SPAN *
ALL ABOUT EVE
AFTER HOURS
SALLY BARKER
MARTIN BARRE
THE BREAKERS *
CLIMAX BLUES BAND
THE ELAINE MORGAN BAND
SHEILA & SHERYL PARKER
DANNY THOMPSON
ZUMZEAUX *

*artists appearing on Friday night

TICKETS	FRI 7–11.30pm	SAT 12–11.30pm	WEEKEND
Before 1 August	£8.00	£13.00	£18.00
After 1 August	£9.00	£15.00	£21.00

Write to Woodworm Records · PO Box 37 · Banbury OX15 4BH
Pay by Access, cheque or postal order. Please enclose SAE.
No mail order after 7 August. Please pay at the gate.

FREE CAMPING AND CAR PARK
THE BEST IN FESTIVAL TOILETS,
(by Royal appointment)

FEEDING AND DRINKING.
BAR BY WADWORTH'S

1990

MY FIRST VISIT TO CROPREDY took place in 1990 and the prevailing memory, for anybody who has been to Cropredy, apart from the state of the toilets, was the weather. The drive down was pleasant, as was the Friday afternoon. It was only as Danny Thompson did his inaugural Cropredy set that the infamous black clouds began to gather - soon, the waterproofs and umbrellas were out, as we all did the annual Cropredy sun dance. However, we weren't concerned as we are used to rain in Britain so we just day-dreamed of our nice warm dry tent.

I was particularly excited about sleeping in a tent as, being only 9 years old, it felt like quite an adventure. Then as the 'Bootleg Beatles' broke into song, all thoughts of rain were forgotten as we were transported back 25 years in one of the best gigs I have ever attended. Then around midnight we all trudged back along the road,

our ankles splashing in water, to our respective fields, singing Beatles songs at the tops of our voices. However, one look at our tent rendered us speechless. Our sleeping bags, and neatly folded pyjamas, were floating in about three inches of water. We spent the night in the car.

The Saturday was quite nice too, even though the rain which fell during Fairport's set forced us to spend another night in the car - didn't put us off, though: - 1990 was our first of eleven consecutive visits.

James Blatchley

1990 CROPREDY FESTIVAL

FRIDAY 17 & SATURDAY 18 AUGUST

CROPREDY nr BANBURY · OXFORDSHIRE

Fairport Convention

with guests RICHARD THOMPSON
JERRY DONAHUE · VIKKI CLAYTON
plus RALPH McTELL*
THE FUREYS & DAVEY ARTHUR
THE BOOTLEG BEATLES*
THE ALBION BAND
BLUES'N'TROUBLE
KIERAN HALPIN
THE JULIAN DAWSON BAND
AVALON*
THE BANANA BAND
Compère DANNY THOMPSON

*artists appearing Friday night

Tickets from Woodworm Records, PO Box 37, Banbury OX15 4BH
Before 1 August : Weekend £20.00, Saturday only £14.00
After 1 August : Weekend £23.00, Saturday only £16.00
Children under 14 admitted FREE
Pay by Access, Visa, cheque or PO. Please send SAE
The best in festival toilets, food and drink
Free camping and car parking
Bar by WADWORTH

I HAVE ALWAYS BEEN a Richard Thompson fan. The fact he was playing on Friday night with his band and listed as a guest for the Saturday Fairport set was what convinced me to make this 'my first Cropredy'.

'*Night Comes In*' had always been one of my favourite songs - especially the long live version. I had just managed to force my way close to the stage during Richard's spot when he began playing it, with an impish grin that seemed to say "you weren't expecting this one were you?"

It was a magnificent version, which seemed to keep rolling on and I never wanted it to end. Shame it's never been released on record, she hinted. **Cath Brierley**

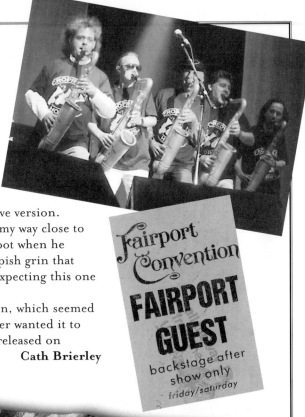

Fairport Convention

CROPREDY 1991 FESTIVAL

FRIDAY 16 & SATURDAY 17 AUGUST
at CROPREDY NR BANBURY • OXON

with **THE RICHARD THOMPSON BAND***
THE STEVE GIBBONS BAND
ALIAS RON KAVANA
WHIPPERSNAPPER
THE POOR MOUTH
STORM*
JAY TURNER
FREEWAY JAM*
BLINDER

**artists appearing Friday night*

Your Master of Ceremonies...
DANNY THOMPSON

The best in festival food, drink
& toilets! Free camping & parking.

TICKETS
Before 1 Aug: SAT £16.00 W'END £24.00
After 1 Aug: SAT £18.00 W'END £27.00
Under 14's admitted free if accompanied

write to WOODWORM RECORDS • PO BOX 37
BANBURY • OXON OX16 8YN • FAX 0869 37142

1992

STOP PRESS
A recent accident has left Ric Sanders temporarily unable to play violin. Many thanks to Chris Leslie for stepping in at short notice in the number 12 shirt.
See page 31 for details.

MY FIRST CROPREDY was something of a big decision. I had been a keen festival goer in my younger days... charging from stage to stage, baking in the sun, eating dubious food, sitting in conditions reminiscent of World War I trenches, generally "roughing it". Now I was older, a little wiser, a mother for heaven's sake with children to think about. But I seen reviews of Cropredy and had been a Fairport fan way back ...and after long debates with my husband we decided to risk it. You wouldn't believe the "contingency plans"... who would watch which set while the other baby sat... games and toys in the tent in case they got bored... clothing for every weather condition imaginable.

What impressed me was just how safe it all was. All contained in one field, with a single focus and everyone so friendly and helpful. It felt like there was a whole field full of baby-sitters! Something which gets forgotten about Cropredy, but which made a big difference to me for quite a few years is the kids' play area. Some of us might be shopping or eating or drinking or watching the stage, but all the time at the top of the field are a dedicated group keeping kids amused, happy and safe with all kinds of entertainment, activities and fun in general. I remember them making dinosaurs one year... and with balloons... even a scratch band one time. I have a distinct memory of Chris Leslie going up and playing with them.

One of my fondest Cropredy memories is sitting at the top of the field, with a veggie curry, waiting for this year's 'sculpture' to be brought to me... the stage a distant shape though the music was still clear and listenable. I looked down and was suddenly struck by just how varied the crowd was... very young kids, bikers, hippies young and old, teenagers, experienced campers. Smartly dressed day visitors, picnickers. Babes in arms and pensioners. It really was (and still is) a miniature village, a real community, "Fairport-convened" for a single weekend.

When my husband arrived with his dish of noodles, I made him sit and look... his words have stayed with me longer than he did. He took in the crowd between us and the stage and said: "It's England isn't it?"

Jackie Oates

Fairport Convention

CELEBRATING 25 YEARS

1992 CROPREDY FESTIVAL

at **CROPREDY** near **BANBURY · OXON**

——— FRIDAY 14 AUGUST ———

FAIRPORT CONVENTION

**SIMON NICOL · DAVE PEGG · RIC SANDERS
MARTIN ALLCOCK · DAVE MATTACKS**
with special guest **JULIANNE REGAN**

•

RICHARD THOMPSON solo

THE WRIGHT BROTHERS

——— SATURDAY 15 AUGUST ———

MORE FAIRPORT!

with special guests **RICHARD THOMPSON
JERRY DONAHUE · DAVE SWARBRICK
ASHLEY HUTCHINGS · RALPH McTELL
VIKKI CLAYTON · BRUCE ROWLAND**
plus a few surprises!

•

**DAVE SWARBRICK AND MARTIN CARTHY
WOLFSTONE · FOUR MEN AND A DOG
THE BACKROOM BOYS** (featuring Jerry Donahue)
SKIN THE PEELER

•

Your compere **DANNY THOMPSON**
And this year . . . decent **TOILETS!**

TICKETS
Available after 20 May
(nostalgia buffs please note:
advance ticket prices
held at 1991 levels!)

**FREE CAMPING
AND PARKING**

Before 1 July
**WEEKEND £24.00
SATURDAY £16.00**

1 July to 5 August
(last date for mail order)
**WEEKEND £27.00
SATURDAY £18.00**

After 5 August
(on the gate only)
**WEEKEND £30.00
SATURDAY £20.00**

from

Woodworm Records

PO BOX 37
**BANBURY
OXON OX16 8YN**
FAX 0869 37142

1993

FRIDAY AUGUST 13, 1993. I should have expected something strange on Friday 13th but wasn't quite prepared for the events of the weekend.
I was at the festival on my own, without knowing anyone onsite, and due to complications in my personal life, feeling pretty low. On arrival I became aware of my campsite neighbours, two men and a woman, because our tents tounched, and as a bee keeper I was intrigued by their flag which had a bee drawn on it. During our first conversation it transpired that this group also kept bees and so common interests were found. They invited me to join them on the field as I was on my own, which made my first night at Cropredy

more sociable than I could have expected. I shall never forget the Leningrad Cowboys viewed from my perch on a stranger's shoulder. Little did I know that a light-hearted wager had been thrown before the male bee keeper to "Chat up the girl in the car in front" as we drove into

the village. Little did they know I was already married and extremely cynical.
Who can resist fatal attraction?
A proposal at Cropredy '95 was followed by a honeymoon at Cropredy '97.
So girls and boys take heed! Be careful who you camp next to at Cropredy. It could change your life!
Elisabeth Langton-Airey

I THINK THE FESTIVAL is always at its most magical at the point late on a hot sunny afternoon when it suddenly and imperceptibly becomes early evening. Something about the light changes and as shadows become more intense, the sky puts on a show that has been worth the wait. I remember this year particularly because it was the one occasion when the company, the music and the venue all conspired to make a moment I would have been happy to die in. I was standing just up the field from the bar with my favourite person, the sky was peach/pink/mauve/blue/turquoise (!) and Everything But the Girl were singing *"I Don't Want to Talk About It"*. For me Cropredy can get no better.
Jane Russ

Woodworm Records proudly presents

Fairport Convention

1993
CROPREDY FESTIVAL
FRIDAY 13 & SATURDAY 14
AUGUST

AT CROPREDY
Nr. BANBURY
OXFORDSHIRE

FRIDAY *(7.15pm till 11.30pm)*

RICHARD THOMPSON
AND DANNY THOMPSON
THE LENINGRAD COWBOYS
CLARION

SATURDAY *(1.00pm till 11.30pm)*

FAIRPORT CONVENTION
with JULIANNE REGAN & VIKKI CLAYTON
plus a few surprise guests!

THE MARTIN BARRE BAND
STOCKTON'S WING
ROBIN WILLIAMSON
FALLEN ANGELS
THE BUTTERMOUNTAIN BOYS

Comperes BOBBY BRAGG & GEOFF HUGHES

And a wealth of good food, drink – and toilets

TICKETS

Before 1st July *(supersaver!)*
WEEKEND £26.00
SATURDAY £17.00

1st July till 5th August
WEEKEND £29.00
SATURDAY £19.00

After 5th August
No mail order, pay on the gate
WEEKEND £32.00
SATURDAY £21.00

Free camping and carparking
Free admission for under 14's
if accompanied

Write to
WOODWORM RECORDS
PO BOX 37, BANBURY
OXON OX16 8YN
enclosing SAE,
or fax 0869 37142

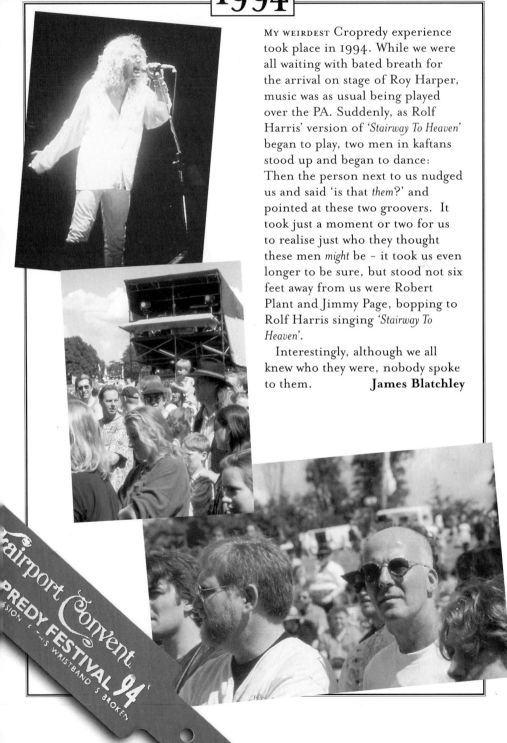

MY WEIRDEST Cropredy experience took place in 1994. While we were all waiting with bated breath for the arrival on stage of Roy Harper, music was as usual being played over the PA. Suddenly, as Rolf Harris' version of '*Stairway To Heaven*' began to play, two men in kaftans stood up and began to dance: Then the person next to us nudged us and said 'is that *them*?' and pointed at these two groovers. It took just a moment or two for us to realise just who they thought these men *might* be - it took us even longer to be sure, but stood not six feet away from us were Robert Plant and Jimmy Page, bopping to Rolf Harris singing '*Stairway To Heaven*'.

Interestingly, although we all knew who they were, nobody spoke to them. **James Blatchley**

CROPREDY FESTIVAL 94

at HOME FARM • CROPREDY
Nr BANBURY • OXFORDSHIRE
FRIDAY 12 AUGUST 7.15pm onwards

LINDISFARNE
ROY HARPER
TOWER STRUCK DOWN

SATURDAY 13 AUGUST 12 noon onwards

Fairport Convention

& special guest **VIKKI CLAYTON**
THE VIN GARBUTT BAND
BLODWYN PIG • HORCH
MAN • SHAVE THE MONKEY
TOO COOL FOR SHORTS
Compere **DANNY THOMPSON**

A wealth of good food, drink ... and toilets

Before July 1st	Weekend £28.00	Saturday £19.00
July 1 - August 4	Weekend £31.00	Saturday £21.00
After August 4*	Weekend £34.00	Saturday £23.00

(*on the gate only) No Friday-only tickets, sorry.
FREE CAMPING Friday & Saturday. Thursday night £5. No camping before Thursday.

FOR TICKETS & INFORMATION, SEND SAE
TO WOODWORM RECORDS, PO BOX 37
BANBURY OX16 8YN or fax 0869 37142

Make cheques/POs payable to Woodworm Records Limited, or send Access/Visa details

MEMORABLE CROPREDYS? What about 1995 - that's when both Roy Wood & Richard Thompson joined Fairport on stage and ran through their most famous songs in turn, with Roy Wood adding a distinctive sound to *'Tear Stained Letter'* before Richard added a jaw-dropping guitar solo to *'I Can Hear The Grass Grow'*. The set finished with Roy Wood coming onto the stage dressed as Santa Claus, singing *'I Wish It Could Be Christmas Every Day'* on a warm August night. Bizarre.

However, a really bizarre moment was the walk back to our tent: Walking along the road, a small group of very drunk people started singing the chorus to *'Blackberry Way'*. Then as those around began to join in, the sound was being carried down the line, until the only sound was a mass drunken choir singing the chorus of *'Blackberry Way'*. Roy Wood should be very proud of that moment. **James Blatchley**

Fairport Convention's CROPREDY FESTIVAL 1995

FRIDAY 11th AUGUST • 7.15 pm
Eden Burning
Kathryn Tickell Band
PROCOL HARUM

SATURDAY 12th AUGUST • 12 noon
Waulk Elektrik
Huw and Tony Williams
The Poozies
The Tribute to Sandy Denny Band
Wild Willy Barrett
The Hamsters
Richard Thompson with Danny Thompson
and

Fairport Convention

plus guests THE ROY WOOD BIG BAND
and Richard Thompson
re Danny Thompson   Sounds by DJ Papa Doc

273

TICKET PRICES		
Before July 1	Weekend £29	Saturday £20
July 1 - August 1	Weekend £32	Saturday £22
After August 1*	Weekend £35	Saturday £24
(*at the gate only)	(No Friday-only tickets)	

Fairport Convention

CROPREDY

AUGUST 11 & 12

FESTIVAL 1995

DAVE & CHRIS PEGG FOR WOODWORM RECORDS PROUDLY PRESENT:

Friday night 7.15 onwards: **Eden Burning**
The Kathryn Tickell Band · PROCOL HARUM
Saturday 12 noon onwards: **Waulk Elektrik**
Huw and Tony Williams · The Poozies
The Tribute to Sandy Denny Band
Wild Willy Barrett · The Hamsters
Richard Thompson with Danny Thompson

And, of course:

Fairport Convention

with guests **The ROY WOOD Big Band**
and **Richard Thompson**
Your compere **Danny Thompson**
Plus a wealth of good food, good drink and toilets...

Before July 1	Weekend **£29.00**	Saturday **£20.00**	*(*at the gate only)* No Friday-only tickets.
July 1 – August 1	Weekend **£32.00**	Saturday **£22.00**	Tickets from the address below. Make cheques/POs payable to Woodworm
After August 1*	Weekend **£35.00**	Saturday **£24.00**	Records Ltd, or send Access/Visa details.

FREE CAMPING *Friday & Saturday. Thursday night £5. No camping before Thursday.*

**SEND SAE TO WOODWORM RECORDS, PO BOX 37
BANBURY, OXON OX16 8YN or FAX 01869 337142**

I'D HAD HEARD Fairport Convention for the first time, in early January '96, when my brother borrowed a copy of The History Of... we'd learned of the festival when they mentioned it on stage, and the next day myself, my brother and his friend made plans to go to Cropredy! Since I was in a wheelchair, and as we only had a one- and two-man tent, I was a bit worried about how things would work out.

After drinking most of the day, we went over to the concert field to watch Richard Thompson - rather early, so we got to see Edward II's set: they were the most unusual band I had ever seen, with a mixture of traditional folk and reggae on squeeze-boxes and violins. But then when Thompson came on he just blew everyone away, he was fantastic to watch and to listen to, even when the heavens opened and the wind picked up to a near force-5, but no one would move out of the field - we just stayed and got drenched.

Saturday brought us windy weather - great for drying-out clothes and bedding on car doors.

A brief look at the record stall left us £60 lighter, so back to the concert field, just in time to see Joe Brown's set: just imagine a cockney knees-up in a farmer's field you've got the picture. Then on came the lads to start their massive four-hour set. It was the Pegg/Nicol/Sanders/Maart/DM line-up, plus great surprise guests - the only one who sticks in the mind was the brilliant Swarb - a true legend. I'm writing this only a couple of weeks after the 2001 festival which is even now fading from this useless thing on my shoulders... **Paul Tomlinson**

DAVE & CHRIS PEGG FOR WOODWORM RECORDS PROUDLY PRESENT

THE 1996 CROPREDY FESTIVAL

CROPREDY nr BANBURY, OXFORDSHIRE

Friday 9 August 5pm start (gates open 12.30pm) Clarion
Kevin Dempsey & Chris Leslie · Edward II
The Richard Thompson Band

Saturday 10 August 12 noon start (gates open 9.30am)
The King Earl Boogie Band
David Hughes & Gerry Conway
The Atlantic Wave Band · The Hellecasters
Show of Hands · Joe Brown and his band

plus

Fairport Convention

with Dave Swarbrick,
Jerry Donahue and a few surprise guests!

TICKETS from the address below.
Make cheques/POs payable to Woodworm
Records Ltd. or send Access/Visa details.
(∗ pay at gate only) No Friday-only tickets.
FREE CAMPING Friday/Saturday. Thursday
night £5.00. No camping before Thursday.

	Weekend	Saturday
Before July 1	£34.00	£20.00
July 1 - August 1	£37.00	£24.00
After August 1∗	£40.00	£26.00

Tickets & info from **Woodworm Records · PO Box 37 · Banbury**
Oxfordshire OX16 8YN · Fax 01869 337142

CROPREDY IS *not* just about the music, the crowds, the food etc. This year was my return to Cropredy after a couple of years' being unable to attend. Of course I remember Ashley's history of the band, and the songs being played in order. But my overwhelming memory is coming out of my tent on Sunday morning and instead of the feeling that was all over, experiencing the joy of the sunshine on my face... the dragonflies in the reeds... the swans on the canal. Fairport are the ultimate English band and Cropredy the ultimate English setting.

Christine Schofield

One of the things everyone remembers about the 30th anniversary Cropredy is Ashley's 'Greek Chorus' linking narrative:

THE COMMENTARY was written just for Cropredy. They said, "Would you like to do this? Would you like to come up with a linking narration?" I threw myself into it and I was very pleased with what I did: no lesser figure than Simon thought it was brilliant; so I was happy with that. It was the biggest turnout they ever had that year: it sold out: they closed the gates. I think that was the only time that happened.

Ashley Hutchings

I WAS PERSUADED to attend my first Cropredy by family members who had been long standing Fairport fans. Through them I knew about Fairport and Cropredy. Not so my work colleagues. Quite excited to be attending Fairport's thirtieth anniversary celebrations I told them where I was going. The system of office Chinese whispers finally got back to me when someone enquired why I was so excited about spending the weekend at a Chiropody Convention. Feet on the Ledge, anyone?

Rosie Rushforth

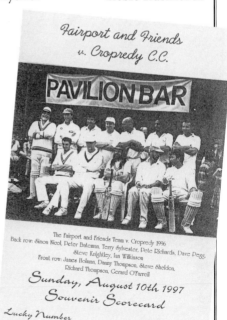

Fairport and Friends v. Cropredy C.C.

PAVILION BAR

The Fairport and Friends Team v. Cropredy 1996
Back row: Simon Nicol, Peter Bateman, Terry Sylvester, Pete Richards, Dave Pegg, Steve Knightley, Ian Wilkinson
Front row: James Holman, Danny Thompson, Steve Sheldon, Richard Thompson, Gerard O'Farrell

Sunday, August 10th 1997
Souvenir Scorecard

Lucky Number

50p

Dave and Chris Pegg for Woodworm Records proudly present

the Cropredy Festival 1997

Featuring Fairport Convention

30TH ANNIVERSARY 67-97

With special guests...
DRESSGANG, *from the USA* Kristina Olsen, *the* Julian Dawson Band, OSIBISA, *the* Saw Doctors *the* NEW BUSHBURY MOUNTAIN DAREDEVILS, *the* Albion Band *from the USA* Tempest, *Huw and* Tony Williams, ELIZA CARTHY *with* THE KINGS OF CALICUTT, John Otway *and* Wild Willy Barrett

THE CROPREDY · FESTIVAL 1998!

FRIDAY
ROY WOOD BIG BAND
EII • RORY McLEOD
FLING • VIKKI CLAYTON BAND
STEVE TILSTON'S STRING THING
SOLSTICE • ANNA RYDER
ON SATURDAY, OF COURSE:
Fairport Convention
PLUS SURPRISE GUESTS!
LOUDON WAINWRIGHT III
HANK WANGFORD BAND • RORY McLEOD • CAT SCRATCH FEVER WAZ • THE TABS *and compère* **DANNY THOMPSON**
WRITE FOR DETAILS TO:
WOODWORM RECORDS
PO BOX 37 BANBURY
OXON OX16 8YN
FAX 01869 337142

FRIDAY & SATURDAY · 14TH & 15TH AUGUST

I HAD WANTED TO GO to Cropredy for years. Friends assured me what a great Festival it was and I knew I would like the music. Every year I was regaled with tales of hot summer's evenings and great electric folk. Sadly I chose to make my first Cropredy one when the weather decided to take a turn for the worse. It was not one of the particularly rainy years, but it was cold. I spent the weekend developing my huddling skills. **Maureen Crossley**

IT WASN'T MY FIRST CROPREDY, not by a long stretch, but for various reasons it was the first time I was able to make a full weekend of it. So it was my first full Cropredy experience. What are now known as The Fairport Supporters were much in evidence: annA rydeR opening the Friday: Steve Tilston alongside Maart in WAZ: David Hughes doing *'The Tango'* during Fairport's set. It was also a year of nostalgia. Chris While is the closest anyone has come to duplicating Sandy's performance and presence: her version of *'Who Knows Where The Time Goes'* as a duet with Simon is a true gem. Then

there was Dave Cousins: I treasure an old single of *'Ringing Down The Years'* and it was a delight to hear it live.
For years 'Cropredy Saturday' has been earmarked in my diary. For the past four years, the full weekend is exclusively set aside and will continue to be so. **Nigel Schofield**

DAViD & CHRiSTiNE PEGG on behalf of WOODWORM RECORDS LiMiTED have great pleasure in announcing for the general DELiGHT & EDiFiCATiON:

CROPREDY FESTiVAL 1998
FRiDAY 14th & SATURDAY 15th AUGUST

>>>> **FRiDAY** proceedings commence 1.00pm <<<<

The ROY WOOD BiG BAND

EII · RORY McLEOD · from Australia FLiNG
The ViKKi CLAYTON BAND · STEVE TiLSON's
STRiNG THiNG · SOLSTiCE · ANNA RYDER

>>>> **SATURDAY** recommencing at 1.00pm <<<<

By popular request to crown the proceedings,

Fairport Convention

...together with some   surprise guests!

LOUDON WAiNWRiGHT III

The HANK WANGFORD BAND · RORY McLEOD
CAT SCRATCH FEVER · WAZ · The TABS... &
your compère beyond compare **Mr DANNY THOMPSON!**

TICKETS

Applications before 15th June	From 16th June until 31st July	From 1st August & on the gate
Weekend £35.00	Weekend £38.00	Weekend £41.00
Saturday £24.00	Saturday £26.00	Saturday £28.00

Children under 12 admitted FREE with paying adult. No Friday-only tickets.
Camping: from Thursday £8.00 per vehicle, from Friday £5.00, Saturday FREE

All of this plus the very best in FESTiVAL COMESTiBLES, a veritable plethora of fine BEVERAGES & the acme of CONVENiENCES!!

Write to WOODWORM RECORDS PO Box 37 Banbury Oxon OX16 8YN or fax 01869 337 142

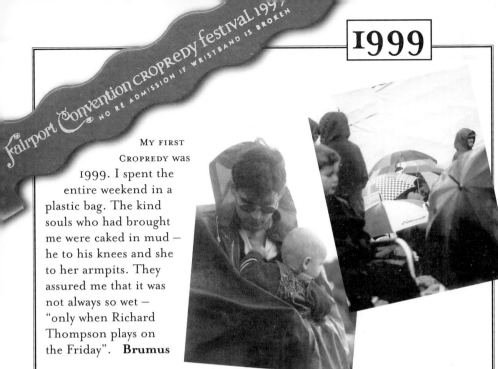

MY FIRST CROPREDY WAS 1999. I spent the entire weekend in a plastic bag. The kind souls who had brought me were caked in mud — he to his knees and she to her armpits. They assured me that it was not always so wet — "only when Richard Thompson plays on the Friday". **Brumus**

THE RAIN HAD STOPPED at about noon. It was hot and sunny and we were down to shorts and t-shirts, but still wearing our wellies. At the bar we met a mate who said he'd just heard of a severe weather warning, headed our way, scheduled to hit in exactly 25 minutes. The sky was blue without a single cloud but as we were going back anyway, to get comfy for Ralph McTell's set, we hurried off. Just a hint of a black cloud in the distance and moving fast. Much to the amazement of everyone around us, we put on our waterproofs and battened down the hatches, just as a rainstorm of biblical proportions hit the site. Ralph had just come on stage, not that we could hear him at this point. The downpour was fierce but short lived. The rest of Ralph's set was wonderful - if moist.

Oh, the joys of inside information...

Mick Toole

A. F. Hiney & Son Ltd., Stockport. 0161-480 4015

Nº 000128

SwarbAid Charity Raffle Appeal

JULY/AUGUST, 1999

ALL PROCEEDS TO DAVE SWARBRICK

★ W I N ★

AN EPIPHONE/GIBSON LES PAUL JUNIOR ELECTRIC GUITAR used by and donated by ROBERT PLANT and signed by ROBERT PLANT and JIMMY PAGE (authenticated by their Management Company)

Promoted by Woodworm Records, P.O. Box 37, Banbury, Oxon. OX16 8YN.

Draw to take place at the Cropredy Festival on Saturday, 14th August, 1999 around 7-45 p.m. Winner if not at the Festival will be notified by post Licenced by Cherwell District Council, No. LA 231

— TICKETS £1.00 EACH

BEFORE ATTENDING my first Cropredy I immersed myself in the music and the programmes of years gone by. The official albums, audience tapes made by friends... a programme which read like a real who's who. Finally in 2000, I made it. Musically Cropredy far exceeded my wildest dreams – great support acts, real surprise guests (Dave Cousins and *'Lay Down'*), Fairport the best I have ever seen them.

Nothing prepared me for the weather, though. Boy, did it rain. We were camped in one of the most distant fields. It seemed quite a trek on the Friday ...but by Saturday afternoon it was a route march, down to the main road, through the village, back up the road and into the top of the field... which I promptly slid all the way down!

We found a pitch... and settled down as Maddy Prior began her set. Determined not to move come hell or high water we stayed there till the last notes of *'Meet on The Ledge'*.

Was it worth the wading?

You bet your life it was!

Tony Crickland

2001

RECOLLECTIONS AND REFLECTION WHILST IRONING.
I am ironing... ironing both 2000 and 2001
Fairport T-shirts. It's a long time since I first
saw them. We were all a lot younger then
and I have lived my adult life with them
and their music alongside. Cropredy is
the celebration with this extended family
of thousands whose names are unknown to me.
Jenni Randall

WARNING
DO NOT
FEED THE ARTISTS

SUNDAY MORNING.
It is hammering with rain, we have three
tents to dismantle and pack together with
their five occupants into the (one) car.
Nobody can bear to leave their tent.
Finally, in best ex-teacher fashion and with
the hazy vision of a hot steamy bath
floating in the back of my mind, I stand
between the tents and give the orders. Lift
that barge and tote that bale, NOW.

Miraculously it happens. As we are
pushing to help the car gain purchase on
the slippery field I turn back to see... a
solitary crew member astride the apex of
the stage canopy (fifty feet up?) bailing
rainwater from the top with a bucket.
What is it they say about there always
being someone worse off than oneself?
Jane Russ

CROPREDY FESTIVAL 2001

AUGUST 9, 10 & 11TH

THURSDAY 9th 5pm-11pm

LONNIE DONEGAN

THE DYLAN PROJECT
featuring Steve Gibbons, PJ Wright, Simon Nicol, Dave Pegg and Gerry Conway

STEVE ASHLEY & FRIENDS

TARRAS

FRIDAY 10th noon-midnight

DE DANNAN from Ireland

MUSAFIR from India

ELIZA CARTHY

SUGARLAND SLIM

CHRIS WHILE & JULIE MATTHEWS

KEITH DONNELLY & GUESTS

WHIRLIGIG from NYC

SANDWITCH from Germany

SATURDAY 11th noon-midnight

Fairport Convention
with special guests
Dave Swarbrick, Beryl & Roger Marriott,
and Vikki Clayton (plus a few surprises!)

BRASS MONKEY

AMOS GARRETT from the USA

FRANCIS DUNNERY & THE GRASS VIRGINS

FIVE FURIOUS FISH

VIKKI CLAYTON & FRIENDS

CHUCKLETRUCK

WADWORTH BEER
Handmade in Devizes

MOJO
The Music Magazine

TICKETS

	Thu/Fri/Sat	Fri/Sat	Sat only
BEFORE JUNE 15	£50.00	£40.00	£26.00
JUNE 15 - JULY 31	£53.00	£43.00	£28.00
FROM AUGUST 1*	£56.00	£46.00	£30.00
Children under 12 FREE if accompanied	£12.00	£8.00	FREE

(*or PAY ON GATE)

CAMPING **
(**Camping charge is PER VEHICLE - bikers and backpackers camp FREE)

INFO AND TICKETS SEND SAE TO:
WOODWORM RECORDS
PO BOX 37 • BANBURY OX16 8YN
FAX 01869 337142

www.fairportconvention.co.uk

2002

MY FIRST CROPREDY...

"Never been??"

"What – you've missed 'em ALL??"

"You don't know what you've been missing Wayney!"

So, this is the year I put it right: the family is alerted that it's to be Croppers rather than Crop-Over; aged tent is unearthed; tickets reserved with Chris and Tracey at Woodworm; sunblock (and waterproofs) ready for packing.

As I edit this booklet in February, anticipation is already building: Leon's Food – what's it like? Lovely real ale close by all weekend – will it be too soporific?? Who will we meet?? Is there fun for nine-year olds too? Shall I take my concertina??

Now, as I'm reading Nigel's tales of great Cropredys of the past and learning so much more about the band who were the soundtrack for my summers of love, back in '68 and '69, and are now finally a major part of my life again, I wait for August: for rainbows, for surprises and sunsets, for Matty, for The Ledge, and for the 20,000 friends that I have yet to meet. See you there.   **Neil Wayne**

ACKNOWLEDGEMENTS

For access to their photographic and memorabilia archives, we thank: Dave Pegg, Ashley Hutchings, Dave Swarbrick, Ian & Steph Rennie at 'Expletive Delighted', Ian Burgess, Ian & Kim, the Mick Toole Poster Archive and all the fans who sent in so many of their tales, pictures and Cropredy reminiscences.

Written and researched by Nigel Schofield, Neil Wayne, and by Fairport fans around the world.

Designed by Mick Toole@PPC.

This book is a companion to the 4-CD/book/poster boxed set entitled 'Fairport unConventioNal', FREE REED FRQCD-35

fairport@free-reed.co.uk
www.free-reed.co.uk/fairport

Made in England by Free Reed Music Belper, Derbyshire DE56 1DD UK